Susanna Warren

A manual of the Litany

with questions for examination

Susanna Warren

A manual of the Litany
with questions for examination

ISBN/EAN: 9783741157370

Manufactured in Europe, USA, Canada, Australia, Japa

Cover: Foto ©Thomas Meinert / pixelio.de

Manufactured and distributed by brebook publishing software
(www.brebook.com)

Susanna Warren

A manual of the Litany

A

MANUAL OF THE LITANY,

WITH

QUESTIONS FOR EXAMINATION.

BY S. W.

AUTHOR OF

"STORIES FOR EVERY SUNDAY IN THE CHRISTIAN YEAR;"
"READINGS ON SOME OF OUR LORD'S PARABLES," &C.

LONDON:

J. AND C. MOZLEY, 6, PATERNOSTER ROW;
MASTERS AND SON, 78, NEW BOND STREET.
1865.

PREFACE.

THIS little Manual has been compiled from the standard Commentaries on the Prayer Book and the Litany, to meet, in the first place, a special case in the Diocese of Exeter, *i. e.* the preparation of candidates in the subjects given out by the Board of Examiners for the examination for the Bishop's Prayer Book Prizes, in the year 1865.

It is hoped, however, that the Manual may be found useful generally for instruction in this portion of the Book of Common Prayer; the more so as there is every probability that the plan which is productive of so much good in the Diocese of Exeter, will in some form or other be adopted before long in Church Schools throughout the country.

In this case the Author proposes to draw up similar manuals on the other Services and Offices of the Church of England.

The little work is largely indebted to the kindness of the Rev. F. Ensor, Rector of Lustleigh, who has afforded much valuable assistance to its Author during its compilation, and has revised it very carefully.

A MANUAL OF THE LITANY.

INTRODUCTION.

THE word Litany means earnest supplication; but it was very soon applied in the Christian Church to a particular form of prayer, in which the priest utters short requests, and the people respond to them; and it is so applied in our Prayer Book. This kind of prayer is very ancient. Some learned men believe that the Jews said Litanies as a part of their synagogue services in the time of our Lord; and without doubt they have been used in both branches of the Christian Church at least from the fourth century.

1. In the Eastern Church. St. Basil affirms that Litanies were read in the Church of Neocæsarea between the time of Gregory Thaumaturgus, (A.D. 250,) and his own time, A.D. 370; and St. Chrysostom (A.D. 397) speaks of the Litanies which had been used while the Church still possessed the miraculous presence of the Spirit in prayer.

2. In the Western Church. St. Ambrose, Bishop of Milan, A.D. 374, wrote a Litany which still bears his name, and which in many points is like the Litany of the English Church. And about A.D. 600, at the time of a great mortality, St. Gregory the Great, out of all the Litanies extant, composed one which has ever since served for a model of this kind of prayer. This was the St. Gregory who sent St. Augustine and a company

of missionaries to convert the Saxon inhabitants of
Britain; and we are told that when they reached
Canterbury they made their entrance into the city
chanting a solemn Litany.

St. Gregory's Litany was called the sevenfold Litany,
because he divided the people into seven classes when
they walked in procession to repeat it. This custom of
saying their prayers while walking in procession through
the streets had come into use two hundred years before,
but on the people growing disorderly it was given up,
and an order put forth that Litanies should for the
future only be used within the walls of the churches.

At first, Litanies were only said in times of public
distress, such as famine, wars, pestilences, earthquakes,
storms, &c., but A. D. 452 Mamercus, Bishop of Vienne,
established the Rogation days, i. e. three days of prayer
preceding Ascension Day, and appointed Litanies to be
used then.

Their use at this season soon became general in the
Western Church. Two centuries later they were said
every month throughout Spain; and so by degrees these
solemn supplications came to be used on Wednesdays
and Fridays in every part of the Church.

The Litany of the English Church is ordered in the
Rubric to be said on Sundays, Wednesdays, and Fridays.
Sunday is the day when the greatest number of people
is present to join in the supplications, and Wednesday
and Friday are the days of our Blessed Lord's betrayal
and crucifixion. It may also be said at other times,
when it shall be commanded by the Ordinary, i. e. the
Bishop of the diocese, or other duly qualified eccle-
siastical officer.

Many ancient forms of Litanies have come down to
us, besides those of St. Ambrose and St. Gregory,
already mentioned. That of the English Church is
like many of these forms, but not exactly the same with
any one of them. It most resembles one in a devotional
book called the Primer, written in English, and used
by private Christians in our country as early as the
fourteenth century, only it is more penitential. It con-

tains more confession of sin, and deeper self-abasement. In the Invocation we call ourselves "miserable sinners," words not contained in that old form. The prayer that God will not remember our offences nor those of our forefathers is new, and so are the words at the beginning of the Supplications, "We *sinners* beseech Thee to hear us."

The Rubric gives no direction about the posture in which the Litany should be said, but our natural feeling suggests that such humble penitential prayers cannot properly be said otherwise than upon our knees. Besides which, the injunction of Queen Elizabeth, A. D. 1559, which still has the force of law, contains these words: "The priests, with others of the choir, shall kneel in the midst of the church, and say or sing plainly and distinctly the Litany, which is set forth in English, with the suffrages following."

When the priest kneels, the people of course must kneel too. The midst of the church is named as the place for saying the Litany, doubtless in allusion to the command of God to the Jews; "Let the Priests, the ministers of the Lord, weep between the porch and the altar, and let them say, Spare Thy people, O Lord," (*Joel*, ii. 17.) And the Litany is still sung or said in that part of the building in Cathedrals, and in many churches.

Our Litany may be divided into four parts. The Invocation, or calling upon God; the Deprecations, or prayers that evil may be averted; the Intercessions, or prayers for others; and the Supplications, or general prayers.

I. THE INVOCATION.

O GOD the Father, of Heaven: have mercy upon us, miserable sinners.

O God the Son, Redeemer of the world: have mercy upon us, miserable sinners.

O God the Holy Ghost, proceeding from the Father and the Son: have mercy upon us, miserable sinners.

O holy, blessed, and glorious Trinity, three Persons
and one God : have mercy upon us, miserable sinners.

Do we ask why we should begin our petitions with
thus calling on the Name of God? We have His own
assurance that it is well pleasing to Him so to do. He
has said, "They shall call on My Name, and I will
hear them;" (*Zech.* xiii. 9.) and, "He shall call on Me,
and I will answer him." (*Psalm* xci. 15.)

1. We call upon *God the Father* Almighty, of
Whom it is said in the Athanasian Creed, "The Father
is made of none : neither created, nor begotten." He
is "the God and Father of our Lord Jesus Christ,"
(1 *Peter,* i. 3.) the Father Who "hath life in Himself;"
(*St. John,* v. 26.) and we may call Him "Abba, Father,"
(*Gal.* iv. 6.) because He hath bestowed such love upon
us that we should be called the sons of God. (1 *St. John,*
iii. 1.) We say God the Father, partly because He is
the Father of all things by creation—"Is He not thy
Father that hath bought thee? hath He not made thee,
and established thee?" (*Deut.* xxxii. 6. See also *Isa.*
lxiv. 3.) partly because He is the Father of all Christians by adoption—"As many as received Him, to them
gave He power to become the sons of God, even to
them that believe on His Name;" (*St. John,* i. 12. See
also *Eph.* i. 5.) but chiefly because He is the Father of
our Lord Jesus Christ. ."Blessed be God, even the
Father of our Lord Jesus Christ, the Father of mercies
and the God of all comfort." (2 *Cor.* i. 3. See also *Eph.*
i. 3.) We say *of Heaven,* because the throne of God—
His chief place of honour—is in Heaven. "Thus saith
the Lord, the Heaven is My throne." (*Isa.* lxvi. 1. See
also *St. Matt.* v. 34.)

2. We call upon *God the Son,* of Whom it is said in
the Athanasian Creed, "The Son is of the Father alone:
not made, nor created, but begotten;" and in the Nicene
Creed, "And in one Lord Jesus Christ, the only begotten Son of God; begotten of His Father before all
worlds; God of God, Light of Light, very God of very
God; begotten, not made, being of one substance
with the Father." He is the Word of God—"In the

beginning was the Word, and the Word was with God, and the Word was God;" (*St. John* i. 1.) the beloved Son of God—"And lo, a voice from heaven, saying, This is My beloved Son;" (*St. Matt.* iii. 17.) the Image of the invisible God—"Who is the Image of the invisible God;" (*Col.* i. 15.) For He is God—"God, of the substance of the Father, begotten before the worlds;" (*Athanasian Creed.*) yet not only God, but man also—"Man, of the substance of His mother, born in the world." (*Athanasian Creed.*) And His Incarnate Name is Jesus, *i.e.* a Saviour—"Thou shalt call His Name Jesus: for He shall save His people from their sins." (*St. Matt.* i. 21.) We call God the Son *Redeemer of the world*, because "He gave Himself for us, that He might redeem us from all iniquity;" (*Titus*, ii. 14.) and because "We have redemption through His Blood, even the forgiveness of sins." (*Col.* i. 14.) This redemption is for the whole world—"He is the propitiation for our sins; and not for ours only, but also for the sins of the whole world." (1 *St. John*, ii. 2. See also *St. John*, i. 29.)

3. We call upon *God the Holy Ghost*, of Whom it is testified in the Athanasian Creed, "The Holy Ghost is of the Father and of the Son: neither made, nor created, nor begotten, but proceeding;" and in the Nicene Creed, "The Holy Ghost, the Lord and Giver of life, Who proceedeth from the Father and the Son, Who with the Father and the Son together is worshipped and glorified." He is the Holy Spirit of God—"And grieve not the Holy Spirit of God:" (*Eph.* iv. 30.) the Comforter, promised by the Lord Jesus when He was going away—"And I will pray the Father, and He shall give you another Comforter, that He may abide with you for ever; even the Spirit of Truth:" (*St. John*, xiv. 16, 17.) the Spirit of adoption—"Ye have received the Spirit of adoption, whereby we cry, Abba, Father." (*Rom.* viii. 15.) That the Holy Ghost proceedeth from the Father we acknowledge. It has ever been held by the Church, and is plainly revealed in Scripture. "When the Comforter is come, Whom I

will send unto you from the Father, even the Spirit of Truth, which proceedeth from the Father, He shall testify of Me." (*St. John*, xv. 26.) That the Holy Ghost also proceedeth from the Son we acknowledge. It is gathered from Scripture in this manner. (1.) Because the Holy Ghost proceedeth from the Father, He is called the Spirit of the Father and the Spirit of God— "It is not ye that speak, but the Spirit of your Father which speaketh in you." (*St. Matt.* x. 20.) "The things of God knoweth no man but the Spirit of God. And we have received not the spirit of the world, but the Spirit which is of God," *i.e.* which proceedeth from God. (1 *Cor.* ii. 11, 12.) Now the Holy Ghost is also called the Spirit of the Son—"God hath sent forth the Spirit of His Son into your hearts:" (*Gal.* iv. 6.) the Spirit of Christ—"Now if any man have not the Spirit of Christ, he is none of His;" (*Rom.* viii. 9. See also 1 *Peter*, i. 11.) the Spirit of Jesus Christ—"I know that this shall turn to my salvation through your prayer, and the supply of the Spirit of Jesus Christ." (*Phil.* i. 19.) He is called the Spirit of God the Father; this proves that He proceedeth from the Father. He is called the Spirit of the Son; this proves that He proceedeth from the Son. (2.) As the Holy Ghost proceedeth from the Father, so the Father sends Him into the world—"The Comforter, which is the Holy Ghost, Whom the Father will send." (*St. John*, xiv. 26.) But the Son also sends the Holy Spirit—"When the Comforter is come, Whom I will send unto you." (*St. John*, xv. 26.) Thus, again, are we taught that "the Holy Ghost is of the Father and of the Son." (*Athanasian Creed.*)

Lastly, we call upon the holy and undivided Trinity, these Three divine Persons in One, for One they are in substance, though Three in Person. "The Godhead of the Father, of the Son, and of the Holy Ghost, is all One; the glory equal, the majesty co-eternal." (*Athanasian Creed.*) And truly the Trinity we worship is most *holy*—"Holy, holy, holy, is the Lord of Hosts;" (*Isa.* vi. 3.) *blessed*—"According to the glorious Gospel of the Blessed God;" (1 *Tim.* i. 11.) and *glorious*—"Who is like Thee, glorious in holiness, fearful in praises, doing wonders?" (*Exodus*, xv. 11.) since God the Father, God the Son, and God the Holy Ghost, are contained therein. "There are Three that bear record in Heaven, the Father, the Word, and the Holy Ghost; and these Three are One." (1 *St. John*, v. 7.) The Persons being separate, they must not be confounded; the substance being one, it must not be divided.

From ignorance or unbelief of these vital truths of our religion, the most fearful heresies have arisen in the Church. We must therefore diligently learn what God has revealed to us respecting Himself, receiving it with a humble mind, and remembering our Saviour's promise; "If any man will do His will, he shall know of the doctrine, whether it be of God." (*St. John*, vii. 17.)

One prayer is mixed with our Invocation. It is a cry for *mercy*. David asked for mercy after his fall. "Have mercy upon me, O Lord, after Thy great goodness." (*Psalm* li. 1.) The blind, (*St. Matt.* xx. 30.) the lepers, (*St. Luke*, xvii. 13.) the afflicted, (*St. Matt.* xv. 22.) all cried to Jesus Christ, "Have mercy." We say it in the true Gospel way, after the manner of the Publican who said, "God be merciful to me, a sinner." (*St. Luke*, xviii. 13.) We own ourselves *miserable sinners*. This is our only plea, for Jesus Christ came not "to call the righteous, but sinners to repentance." (*St. Matt.* ix. 13.) Not that He looks favourably on sin; no, it is the "abominable thing that He hates;" (*Jer.* xliv. 4.) but since we are sinners, He will have us confess it, that on our true repentance He may forgive us. "He that covereth his sins shall not prosper; but whoso confesseth and forsaketh them shall have mercy." (*Prov.* xxviii. 13.)

The people repeat the Invocations after the minister, every voice joining in the cry for mercy. Afterwards they leave it to the priest to set forth all their wants to God, only declaring their assent to every petition when he has uttered it.

After the Invocation to the Holy Trinity, Invocations

to the Saints were introduced into the Litanies of the Western Church about the eighth century. These, however, were left out at the Reformation, as without warrantry from Scripture, and contrary to the usage of the Church in its earliest and purest days.

II. THE DEPRECATIONS.

THE Deprecations, or prayers against evil, are addressed to our Lord Jesus Christ, and are all founded upon the one petition in the Lord's Prayer, "Deliver us from evil."

"Remember not, Lord, our offences, nor the offences of our forefathers; neither take Thou vengeance of our sins: spare us, good Lord, spare Thy people whom Thou hast redeemed with Thy most precious blood, and be not angry with us for ever.
"Spare us, good Lord."

First we pray our Lord Jesus Christ *not* to *remember* our own offences; to pass by what we have done, to "blot out our iniquities." (*Psalm* li. 9.) We say with the prophet, "Be not wroth very sore, O Lord; neither remember iniquity for ever;" (*Isa.* lxiv. 9.) with the Psalmist, "Remember not the sins and offences of my youth." (*Psalm* xxv. 6.) Nay, we make our petition in the very words of Scripture: "O remember not our old sins, but have mercy upon us, and that soon;" (*Psalm* lxxix. 8.) "Spare Thy people, O Lord, and give not Thine heritage to reproach;" (*Joel,* ii. 17.) and encouraged by Scripture promise, "Their sins and their iniquities will I remember no more." (*Heb.* viii. 12.) See also *Isa.* xliii. 25; *Jer.* l. 20.

Next we ask Him not to remember *the offences of our forefathers;* because, though at the judgment day the son will not bear the iniquity of the father, yet in this world children do suffer for their parents' sins. Thus at the first destruction of Jerusalem the Jews then living underwent a punishment which their forefathers' sins helped to draw down. Jeremiah said, " Our fathers have sinned, and are not; and we have borne their iniquities." (*Lam.* v. 7.) Thus the mass of human wickedness swells and increases year by year, calling down vengeance upon sinful nations. "We have sinned with our fathers; we have done amiss, and dealt wickedly;" (*Psalm* cvi. 6.) therefore we ask our Lord Jesus to *spare* us. And on what ground? Even because He has redeemed us with His most precious Blood—"Ye were not redeemed with corruptible things, ... but with the precious Blood of Christ." (1 *Pet.* i. 18, 19.) We ask Him not to be *angry with us for ever*, but to send us chastisement in this life, if such be good for us, not punishment in the next.

"From all evil and mischief; from sin, from the crafts and assaults of the devil; from Thy wrath, and from everlasting damnation :
"Good Lord, deliver us."

Evil and mischief seem here to mean the ills of this life—"All adversities that may happen to the body." (*Collect for the Second Sunday in Lent.*) From these we may ask to be kept, if only we do so in full submission to God's will. Thus Jacob prayed, "Deliver me, I pray Thee, from the hand of my brother, from the hand of Esau;" (*Gen.* xxxii. 11.) and Hezekiah besought the Lord to save him when threatened by Sennacherib. (2 *Kings,* xix. 14–19. See also *Psalm* xci. 3–6.) If evil and mischief threaten the body, what threatens the soul? *Sin,* to which since the Fall, man has ever been prone. And what is sin? "Sin is the transgression of the law." (1 *St. John,* iii. 4.) Sin is something done, said, or willed, against the eternal law of God, and therefore most hateful in His sight—"All that do unrighteously are an abomination unto the Lord thy God." (*Deut.* xxv. 16.) We are liable to fall into sin from our own weakness, and the corruption of our nature. "The evil that I would not, that I do. When I would do good, evil is present with me." (*Rom.* vii. 19, 21. See also *Gal.*

v. 17.) "By reason of the frailty of our nature we
cannot always stand upright." (*Collect for the Fourth
Sunday after Epiphany.*) And also *the Devil* leads us
into it. He is cunning as a serpent—"That old
serpent called the Devil and Satan, which deceiveth the
whole world;" (*Rev.* xii. 9.) and so he tempts us by
his *crafts*, hiding from us the evil of what he wants us
to do. Thus he "beguiled Eve through his subtlety."
(2 *Cor.* xi. 3. See also 1 *Tim.* ii. 14.) But he is also
like a roaring lion, fierce and strong: "Your adversary,
the devil, as a roaring lion, walketh about seeking
whom he may devour;" (1 *Peter*, v. 8.) and thus he
drives us into sin, by *assaults*, through sudden surprise,
and dread of suffering. In whichever way he wars
against the soul, he does it by suggesting evil thoughts;
therefore we pray to be defended "from all evil thoughts
which may assault and hurt the soul." (*Collect for the
Second Sunday in Lent.*)

What is the consequence of sin? God's *wrath*.
"The wrath of God is revealed from Heaven against
all ungodliness and unrighteousness of men." (*Rom.* i.
18. See also *Eph.* v. 6.) It is now' hanging over the
wicked, and if repentance and God's mercy turn it not
away, it will abide upon them, (*St. John*, iii. 36.) and
issue in *everlasting damnation*—"The angels shall come
forth and sever the wicked from among the just, and
shall cast them into the furnace of fire: there shall be
weeping and gnashing of teeth;" (*St. Matt.* xiii. 49, 50.)
"The fire that never shall be quenched; where their
worm dieth not, and the fire is not quenched." (*St. Mark*,
ix. 43, 44.)

"From all blindness of heart; from pride, vain-
glory, and hypocrisy; from envy, hatred, and malice,
and all uncharitableness:
"Good Lord, deliver us."

When the *heart* is *blind*, it can neither discern God
nor spiritual things. This miserable state is the result
of shutting the eyes against the truth, and sinning
recklessly. Thus the Jews in our Saviour's time

turned away from the Light of the world—"This is the condemnation, that light is come into the world, and men loved darkness rather than light, because their deeds were evil;" (*St. John*, iii. 19.) and so they passed into a state of darkness. "If thine eye be evil, thy whole body shall be full of darkness." (*St. Matt.* vi. 23. See also 1 *St. John*, ii. 11., and 2 *St. Peter*, i. 9.) It is the just punishment of sin—"They received not the love of the truth, that they might be saved. And for this cause God shall send them strong delusion, that they should believe a lie;" (2 *Thess.* ii. 10, 11. See also *Isaiah*, xliv. 18; *St. Matt.* xiii. 14, 15.) as well as the cause of fresh sin—"That ye henceforth walk not as other Gentiles walk, in the vanity of their mind, having the understanding darkened, being alienated from the life of God through the ignorance that is in them, because of the blindness of their heart; who, being past feeling, have given themselves over unto lasciviousness, to work all uncleanness with greediness." (*Eph.* iv. 17–19.) And therefore the Psalmist prays, "Open Thou mine eyes." (*Psalm* cxix. 18.) *Pride* consists in thinking too much of ourselves and our gifts, without ascribing all that is good in us to God. Thus Nebuchadnezzar said, "Is not this great Babylon, that I have built for the house of the kingdom by the might of my power, and for the honour of my majesty?" (*Daniel*, iv. 30.) He was punished immediately; for God "plenteously rewardeth the proud doer." (*Psalm* xxxi. 26.) Pride is very displeasing to Him—"Every-one that is proud in heart is an abomination unto the Lord;" (*Prov.* xvi. 5.) for "He is a jealous God." (*Exod.* xx. 5.) and "will not give His glory to another." (*Isaiah*, xlviii. 11.) *Vain-glory* is a sin which comes from the same root as pride. It consists in preferring the praise of man to the praise of God, and leads to boasting and talking of self. Hezekiah yielded to vain-glory when he showed the Babylonian messengers all his treasures; (2 *Kings*, xx. 12–15.) and Herod, when he received his people's impious praise. (*Acts.* xii. 21–23.) But St. Paul warns us against it—"Let nothing be done through strife or vain-glory." (*Phil.* ii. 3. See also *Gal.* v. 26.) *Hypocrisy* is pretending to be better and more religious than we are; a subtle sin, but very dangerous. Our Lord warns us against hypocrisy in almsgiving, (*St. Matt.* vi. 1–4.) in prayer, (*Verses* 5, 6.) and in fasting. (*Verses* 16–18.) He condemns the Pharisees for it—"Beware ye of the leaven of the Pharisees, which is hypocrisy." (*St. Luke,* xii. 1. See also *St. Matt.* xxiii. 13–33.) *Envy* is repining at the good or happiness of others. Thus Cain envied Abel the favour of God shown in the acceptance of Abel's offering; (*Gen.* iv. 4, 5.) and the patriarchs, "moved with envy," (of their father's love to him,) "sold Joseph into Egypt." (*Acts,* vii. 9.) The heathen world was "full of envy;" (*Rom.* i. 29.) but God will not have His people "envying one another." (*Gal.* v. 26.) *Hatred* is anger against another person, deeply rooted and fixed in the soul. It is set down among the works of the flesh, (*Gal.* v. 20.) and it hinders us from loving God. "If a man say, I love God, and hateth his brother, he is a liar; for he that loveth not his brother, whom he hath seen, how can he love God, whom he hath not seen?" (1 *St. John,* iv. 20.) Hatred leads on to *malice,* or plotting and planning evil against our neighbour. Thus the rulers of the Jews, hating our Lord, laid snares for Him. "They watched Him, and sent forth spies, which should feign themselves just men, that they might take hold of His words, that so they might deliver Him into the power and authority of the governor." (*St. Luke,* xx. 20. See also *St. John,* xi. 47–53.) But the Christian must put off malice— "But now ye also put off all these; anger, wrath, malice." (*Col.* iii. 8. See also 1 *St. Peter,* ii. 1.) Envy, hatred, and malice, are three evil branches which grow from one root, *uncharitableness,* or want of love to our neighbour. From it, in whatever form it may show itself, we pray to be delivered; for love to our neighbour is the very test by which to judge the spiritual life—"We know that we have passed from death unto life, because we love the brethren. He that loveth not his brother abideth in death." (1 *St. John*, iii. 14.)

"From fornication, and all other deadly sin; and from all the deceits of the world, the flesh, and the devil:

"Good Lord, deliver us."

By *fornication* is meant the works of the flesh, of which St. Paul speaks, *Gal.* v. 19–21, saying that they which do such things shall not inherit the kingdom of God. Such sin is very awful in a Christian, because his body is the temple of God. "Ye are the temple of the living God;" (2 *Cor.* vi. 16. See also 1 *Cor.* vi. 19.) and "If any man defile the temple of God, him shall God destroy." (1 *Cor.* iii. 17.)

It is a *deadly sin*, and there are other deadly sins from which also we pray to be delivered. In fact, all sin wilfully committed against light and knowledge is deadly sin, since it puts us at once out of a state of grace. "There is a sin unto death." (1 *John*, v. 16. See also *Psalm* xix. 13.) The *world*, the *flesh*, and the *devil*, are the three powers of evil we renounced at our Baptism; but they are ever striving to get possession of us again, and too often they prevail through their *deceits*. The devil is full of deceits—"We are not ignorant of his devices." (2 *Cor.* ii. 11.) "Satan himself is transformed into an angel of light." (2 *Cor.* xi. 14.) He invents many excuses for sin, explains away its guilt, and sets it in the most attractive light. The world is full of deceits. It would make us believe its pomps and glories to be real, whereas they are only a vain show. "Man walketh in a vain shadow, and disquieteth himself in vain." (*Psalm* xxxix. 7. See also *St. James*, iv. 14; 1 *Peter*, i. 24.) The flesh is full of deceits, for it is always trying to persuade us that we require one indulgence or another, whereas, our only safety is in "mortifying the deeds of the body," (*Rom.* viii. 13.) in "keeping under the body, and bringing it into subjection." (1 *Cor.* ix. 27.)

2

"From lightning and tempest; from plague, pestilence, and famine; from battle and murder, and from sudden death:

"Good Lord, deliver us."

When the cause is removed, we may dare to hope the consequences will be prevented. And thus, after praying to be delivered from sin in its manifold forms, we pray against those judgments which God commonly sends as the punishment of sin. And first—

Lightning and tempest are ministers of God's wrath. After describing a thunder-storm, Elihu says, "He causeth it to come, whether for correction, or for His land, or for mercy." (*Job*, xxxvii. 13. See also 1 *Sam*. xii. 16–20.) Thunder-storms cause destruction of property, and death, even in our own land; but in tropical countries they are far more awful. Sometimes whole districts are laid waste in the West Indies by hurricanes or tornadoes, which kill the people, throw down the houses, and lay waste the plantations. And the Indian Ocean is visited by cyclones, that is whirlwinds, which draw up the water of the ocean and pour it down again in water-spouts. In November, 1864, the eastern coast of India was visited by a cyclone, which swept over seven hundred and thirty-two square miles of country; destroying many towns and villages, and more than 10,000 people. *Plague* and *pestilence* are violent epidemic diseases. In hot countries they sweep off numbers of people by sudden painful death. England used to be visited by the Plague. In 1665 it raged in London, so that 100,000 people perished from it in one year. God has, however, mercifully kept us from it since. But our country has suffered, within the last thirty years, from visitations of the Asiatic Cholera, a severe and malignant disease. *Famine*, or dearth of food, is also a calamity little known in our rich and fruitful country. In 1845, however, there was scarcity in England, and famine in Ireland, from bad harvests and the loss of the potato crops, through a new disease. *Battle* or war brings great misery with it, especially on the country which it desolates. There have been no battles in England since the Civil War in the reign of Charles I.; (A. D. 1642.) but the Crimean War, (A. D. 1854 and 1855) showed us in some measure the awfulness of this scourge of God. The dreadful war raging of late in North America, shows it yet more plainly. Plague and pestilence, famine and war, are God's sore judgments on a guilty land—"Thus saith the Lord God; how much more when I send my four sore judgments upon Jerusalem, the sword, and the famine, and the noisome beast, and the pestilence, to cut off from it man and beast?" (*Ezekiel,* xiv. 21.) We pray to be delivered from them, and also from *murder,* or death at the hands of a fellow creature, or any *sudden death.* The old Litanies said, "a sudden and unprovided (or as we should say unprepared) death." Christians should be ready whenever their master calls for them; they must take care not to leave the work of repentance to be done at the brink of the grave. Still death is so fearful and momentous, that we may well pray that it come not upon us without a season of special preparation.

"From all sedition, privy conspiracy, and rebellion; from all false doctrine, heresy, and schism; from hardness of heart, and contempt of Thy Word and Commandment:
"Good Lord, deliver us."

Whatever may be the form of government in a country, and whatever the personal character of its rulers, the inhabitants of that country owe it the strictest obedience; for "the powers that be are ordained of God." (*Rom.* xiii. 1.) Our Lord Jesus said, "Render unto Cæsar the things that are Cæsar's;" (*St. Matt.* xxii. 21.) though the Cæsar referred to was prince of a foreign country, whose armies had conquered Judea, and a cruel heathen tyrant. Three sins against the state are mentioned here. *Sedition,* or unlawful gatherings of the people against their rulers; *privy conspiracy,*

or secret plottings against them; and *rebellion*, or open
resistance of their authority. And all are in reality
sins against God, who has said to us, "Submit your-
selves to every ordinance of man for the Lord's sake ;"
(1 *St. Pet.* ii. 13.) and, "Whosoever resisteth the power,
resisteth the ordinance of God; and they that resist
shall receive to themselves damnation." (*Rom.* xiii. 2.
See also *Tit.* iii. 1.)

Next three sins against the Church are named. *False
doctrine* or teaching, whether in the way of adding to
the truth, or diminishing from it. This is sinful, for
God has revealed the Truth to us, and we should
receive it humbly and keep it faithfully. " Ye shall
not add unto the word which I command you, neither
shall ye diminish ought from it." (*Deut.* iv. 2.) St.
Peter prophesies, " There shall be false teachers among
you, who privily shall bring in damnable heresies, even
denying the Lord that bought them, and bring upon
themselves swift destruction." (2 *St. Pet.* ii. 1.) And
St. Paul says of such, " I would they were even cut off
which trouble you." (*Gal.* v. 12.) *Heresy*, which is
false doctrine wilfully and pertinaciously held. It is
either putting falsehood for the truth, or corrupting the
truth, or denying the truth. Of heretics St. Paul said
to Titus, " A man that is an heretic, after the first and
second admonition reject, knowing that he that is such
is subverted, and sinneth, being condemned of himself."
(*Tit.* iii. 10, 11.) *Schism*, or division, which ends in a
separation from the communion of the Church. This
is the result either of false doctrine or of party feelings.
St. Paul exhorts the Corinthians, " Now I beseech you,
brethren, by the name of our Lord Jesus Christ, that
ye all speak the same thing, and that there be no divisions (schisms, *marginal reading*) among you." (1 *Cor.* i.
10.) And to the Romans he says, " Mark them which
cause divisions and offences contrary to the doctrine
which ye have learned ; and avoid them." (*Rom.* xvi.
17. See also 1 *Cor.* iii. 3.) On the eve of His Passion our Lord prayed for the unity of His Church,
" That they all may be one ; as Thou, Father, art in

Me, and I in Thee, that they also may be one in Us."
(*St. John*, xvii. 21.) Alas! through these sins of false
doctrine, heresy, and schism, it is in the present day
fearfully divided!

When man goes on in the way of his own heart, that
heart becomes hard. So it was with the children of
Israel in the days of the Captivity—"They are impudent
children and stiff-hearted." (*Ezek.* ii. 4. See also
chap. iii. 7.) *Hardness of heart* is God's judgment upon
unrepented sin. Thus, after Pharaoh had hardened
his heart, (*Exod.* viii. 15 and 32.) it is said that God
hardened his heart. (*Exod.* ix. 12; x. 20; xi. 10.)
Contempt of God's Word and Commandment, is the lowest
depth of iniquity into which indulged sin can lead a
man, and the natural result of that indulgence. It
draws down the wrath of God and His judgments.
"Because I have called, and ye refused; I have
stretched out My hand, and no man regarded; but ye
have set at nought all My counsel, and would none of
My reproof; I also will laugh at your calamity; I will
mock when your fear cometh; when your fear cometh
as desolation, and your destruction cometh as a whirl-
wind; when distress and anguish cometh upon you."
(*Prov.* i. 24–27.)

" By the mystery of Thy Holy Incarnation; by Thy
Holy Nativity and Circumcision; by Thy Baptism,
Fasting, and Temptation:
" Good Lord, deliver us."
" By Thine Agony and Bloody Sweat: by Thy Cross
and Passion: by Thy precious Death and Burial: by
Thy glorious Resurrection and Ascension; and by the
coming of the Holy Ghost:
" Good Lord, deliver us."

Every action of our Lord Jesus Christ, being the
action of God, is of infinite value. We cannot tell how
wonderfully great every one of them is, but we may
plead them in turn before Him; we may ask Him for
the sake of what He did or suffered for us then, to

deliver us now. We say, *By the mystery of Thy Holy
Incarnation,* because when the Word was made flesh,
or Incarnate, and thus the nature of God and the
nature of man were united in the Person of Jesus
Christ, our nature was cleansed. "The Word was
made flesh, and dwelt among us." (*St. John,* i. 14.) We
say *By Thy Nativity,* because through His birth into the
visible world, we are born into the invisible world,
and become sons of God. "God sent forth His Son,
made of a woman, made under the Law, to redeem them
that were under the Law, that we might receive the
adoption of sons." (*Gal.* iv. 4, 5.) We plead Christ's
Circumcision, because it was His first act of obedience
to the Law for man, and also because He then first shed
His precious Blood and received the Name of Jesus,
earnest of our salvation—"When eight days were accomplished for the circumcising of the child, His Name
was called Jesus:" (*St. Luke,* ii. 21.) His *Baptism,* for
He then sanctified the element of water to the mystical
washing away of sin : His *Fasting* and *Temptation,*
because through it He learned sympathy with our infirmities—"We have not an high priest which cannot
be touched with the feeling of our infirmities ; but was
in all points tempted like as we are, yet without sin ;"
(*Heb.* iv. 15.) and acquired power to help us in temptation—"For in that He Himself hath suffered being
tempted, he is able to succour them that are tempted."
(*Heb.* ii. 18.)

We plead the *Agony and Bloody Sweat,* because by
treading alone the winepress of God's vengeance, our
Lord released us from His wrath. We plead Christ's
Cross and Passion, because by it He bore the penalty of
our sin and paid our ransom. "Who His own self bare
our sins in His own body on the tree ; that we, being
dead to sin, should live unto righteousness." (1 *St. Pet.*
ii. 24.) See also *Heb.* ix. 28. We plead His *Death
and Burial,* because through death He destroyed "him
that hath the power of death, that is the devil :" (*Heb.*
ii. 14. See also *Col.* ii. 15.) His *Glorious Resurrection,*
for He was "raised again for our justification:" (*Rom.*

iv. 25.) His *Ascension*, for He has borne our human nature unto the highest heavens, and there maketh intercession for us—"We have a great High Priest that is passed into the heavens, Jesus the Son of God." (*Heb.* iv. 14.) "Wherefore He is able to save them to the uttermost that come unto God by Him, seeing He ever liveth to make intercession for them." (*Heb.* vii. 25.) Lastly, we plead *by the coming of the Holy Ghost*, for it was the crowning act of our Lord's goodness to man. He said, "It is expedient for you that I go away; for if I go not away the Comforter will not come unto you; but if I depart I will send Him unto you." (*St. John*, xvi. 7.)

"In all time of our tribulation; in all time of our wealth; in the hour of death, and in the day of judgement:
    "Good Lord, deliver us."

We here name four seasons when we specially need help and deliverance from God. The first is in time of *tribulation*. Now tribulation means strictly the process by which corn is freed from the husks or chaff with a threshing instrument. Here the word means affliction or trouble, by means of which God separates off what is low and base from His people, of whom He says, "O My threshing, and the corn of My floor." (*Isa.* xxi. 10.) Still a time of tribulation is a time when we need God's special help; for if it does not make us better, it will make us worse. So it was with the Jews—"Why should ye be stricken any more? ye will revolt more and more." (*Isa.* i. 5. See also *Jer.* v. 3.) 2. *In time of our wealth*, or prosperity, we need help, then, because it is of the very nature of riches, and the pleasures and comforts they bring with them, to draw our hearts from God. Agur prayed against riches, "Lest," he said, "I be full, and deny Thee, and say Who is the Lord?" (*Prov.* xxx. 9.) And the children of Israel forsook God in the time of their wealth. "Jeshurun waxed fat and kicked; thou art waxen fat, thou art grown thick, thou art covered with fatness; then he forsook God which made him, and lightly esteemed the Rock of his salvation." (*Deut.* xxxii. 15. See also *Neh.* ix. 25, 26.) Riches are, in the tempter's hand, instruments to lead us to forget God, or to think we can do without Him. "The deceitfulness of riches choke the word;" (*St. Matt.* xiii. 22.) and our Lord has said, "How hardly shall they that have riches enter into the kingdom of God!" (*St. Mark,* x. 23.) Therefore St. Paul said to Timothy, "Charge them that are rich in this world, that they be not high minded, nor trust in uncertain riches, but in the living God." (1 *Tim.* vi. 17.) 3. *In the hour of death;* for though Christ came to "deliver them who through fear of death were all their lifetime subject to bondage," (*Heb.* ii. 15.) yet it is a solemn and momentous hour. Past sin then presses very heavily on the conscience—"The sting of death is sin;" (1 *Cor.* xv. 56.) and Satan makes his last assault upon the soul, doing his utmost to pluck it away from God. When our Lord was going from the Garden of Gethsemane to His death, He said to His persecutors, "This is your hour, and the power of darkness." (*St. Luke,* xxii. 53.) While the Lord Jesus hung upon the Cross the devil did his worst against Him; and we too must expect in the hour of death to wrestle "Not against flesh and blood, but against principalities, against powers, against the rulers of the darkness of this world, against 'wicked spirits,' (*marginal reading*) in high places." (*Eph.* vi. 12.) 4. *In the day of judgment:* "For we must all appear before the judgment-seat of Christ, that everyone may receive the things done in his body, according to that he hath done, whether it be good or bad." (2 *Cor.* v. 10.) Prophets and Apostles tell us alike of the awfulness of that day, "A day of wrath, a day of trouble and distress, a day of wasteness and desolation, a day of darkness and gloominess, a day of clouds and thick darkness." (*Zeph.* i. 15.) See also *Amos,* v. 18. The cry then will be, "The great day of His wrath is come, and who shall be able to stand?" (*Rev.* vi. 17.) "And if the righteous scarcely be saved, where shall the ungodly and the sinner appear?" (1 *St. Pet.* iv. 18.) Well may we say, "In the day of judgement, good Lord, deliver us."

III.—THE INTERCESSIONS.

INTERCESSION means "asking for others." We have great encouragement to this kind of prayer. It is doing on earth what our Lord Jesus is doing at the right hand of the Father—"He ever liveth to make intercession for us;" (*Heb.* vii. 25.) and when we intercede for our brethren, it brings us very near to Him and to them. St. Paul exhorts us that intercessions be made for all men. (1 *Tim.* ii. 1.) Some of our Lord's chief miracles were wrought at the beseeching, *i. e.* intercession, of others; as the healing of the nobleman's son; (*St. John,* iv. 45–53.) of the centurion's servant; (*St. Luke,* vii. 2–10.) Jairus' daughter; (*St. Luke,* viii. 41–56.) and the daughter of the woman of Canaan. (*St. Matt.* xv. 22–28.) And the parable of the friend at midnight teaches us how God hears earnest intercessory prayer. (*St. Luke,* xi. 5–8.) The intercessions are addressed to our Lord Jesus Christ, as were the Deprecations.

"We sinners do beseech Thee to hear us, O Lord God; and that it may please Thee to rule and govern Thy Holy Church universal in the right way:
"We beseech Thee to hear us, good Lord."

We intercede first for Christ's *Holy Church Universal,* the holy Catholic and Apostolic Church of our Creeds, the fifth kingdom of Daniel's vision—"And in the days of these kings shall the God of Heaven set up a kingdom which shall never be destroyed." (*Dan.* ii. 44.) We pray our Lord Jesus Christ to *rule and govern* the Church, because He is her Head—"Christ is the Head of the Church;" (*Eph.* v. 23.) and her King—"There was given Him dominion and glory and a kingdom." (*Dan.* vii. 13.) "I appoint unto you a kingdom, as My

Father hath appointed unto Me." (*St. Luke*, xxii. 29.)
We ask with confidence, because He has promised that
the gates of hell shall not prevail against it; (*St. Matt.*
xvi. 18.) and we should ask most earnestly, because the
salvation of so many souls depends on the purity and
wise governance of the Church.

After praying for the universal Church, in whose
good we are most concerned, since she is the common
mother of all Christians, we turn to the wants of our
own Church; and first we commend to God our Queen.

"That it may please Thee to keep and strengthen in
the true worshipping of Thee, in righteousness and
holiness of life, Thy servant Victoria, our most gracious
Queen and Governour:

"We beseech Thee to hear us, good Lord.

"That it may please Thee to rule her heart in Thy
faith, fear, and love, and that she may evermore have
affiance in Thee, and ever seek Thy honour and glory:

"We beseech Thee to hear us, good Lord.

"That it may please Thee to be her defender and
keeper, giving her the victory over all her enemies:

"We beseech Thee to hear us, good Lord."

It is plain from Holy Scripture that rulers and
governors are set over us by God. "By Me," saith
the Wisdom of God, "kings reign and princes decree
justice." (*Prov.* viii. 15. See also *Dan.* ii. 21; *Rom.*
xiii. 1.) Hence it is our duty to pray for them, and it
is our wisdom also, for the godliness and well-doing of
a nation depends very much on its rulers. The books
of Kings and Chronicles teach us that when the kings
of Judah and Israel were wicked, the people also fell
into wickedness. Jeroboam "did sin," and "made
Israel to sin;" (1 *Kings*, xiv. 16.) and when Manasseh
did evil in the sight of the Lord, he "made Judah and
the inhabitants of Jerusalem to err and to do worse
than the heathen." (2 *Chron.* xxxiii. 9.) For the sake of
the nation, therefore, and for our own sakes, we should
pray for our Queen. Besides, kings and princes have

special temptations from their high station, and therefore more than others require the help of our prayer. But God "giveth salvation unto kings;" (*Psalm* cxliv. 10.) and we must beseech Him to do so, remembering that when St. Paul bids us pray for all men, he adds, "For kings, and for all that are in authority; that we may lead a quiet and peaceable life in all godliness and honesty." (1 *Tim.* ii. 2.)

We offer up three prayers for our Queen—1. That she may be kept in the right faith, in the *true worshipping of God.* 2. That God may rule her heart, and that she may have affiance (*i. e.* trust) in Him. "The king's heart is in the hand of the Lord." (*Prov.* xxi. 1.) 3. That she may be protected against her enemies, and be victorious over them. God made a promise to David, "I will subdue all thine enemies;" (1 *Chron.* xvii. 10.) and He fulfilled it—"Thou hast given victory unto kings, and hast delivered David Thy servant from the peril of the sword." (*Psalm* cxliv. 10.)

"That it may please Thee to bless and preserve Albert Edward Prince of Wales, the Princess of Wales, and all the Royal Family:

"We beseech Thee to hear us, good Lord."

We are at present happy under the government of our gracious Queen; but since a crown is no safeguard from the hand of death, and the security of the government commonly depends upon the royal family, we pray for them, and chiefly for the heir apparent, the Prince of Wales, who, if God preserves him, will hereafter be our King. When Darius, King of Persia, asked the prayers of the Jews for himself, he asked them also for his sons. (*Ezra,* vi. 10.) The petition for the royal family was introduced into the Litany in the reign of James I.

"That it may please Thee to illuminate all Bishops, Priests, and Deacons, with true knowledge and understanding of Thy Word; and that both by their preaching and living they may set it forth and show it accordingly:

"We beseech Thee to hear us, good Lord."

The ministry of Christ, in the threefold order of *Bishops, Priests,* and *Deacons,* have their commission straight from Him—"As My Father sent Me," He said to His Apostles, "even so send I you." (*St. John,* xx. 21. See also *Eph.* iv. 8, 11, 12.) Our Lord Jesus brought salvation from Heaven; His ministers convey it to men. The Holy Ghost hath made them overseers over the flock, "to feed the Church of God which He hath purchased with His own blood;" (*Acts,* xx. 28.) and "They watch for our souls as they that must give account." (*Heb.* xiii. 7.) Therefore we are bound to pray for them, (as we are directed in the Collects for the Third Sunday in Advent and for St. Matthias' and St. Peter's days,)—1. That they may be illumined or enlightened with the *knowledge and understanding of God's Word*—"The entrance of Thy Word giveth light." (*Psalm* cxix. 130.) 2. That they may set forth this light by their *preaching* and *living, i. e.* by sound teaching and a holy life. To this St. Paul exhorted Titus—"Speak thou the things which become sound doctrine; in all things showing thyself a pattern of good works." (*Titus,* ii. 1, 7.)

"That it may please Thee to endue the Lords of the Council, and all the Nobility, with grace, wisdom, and understanding:

"We beseech Thee to hear us, good Lord."

"That it may please Thee to bless and keep the Magistrates; giving them grace to execute justice, and to maintain truth:

"We beseech Thee to hear us, good Lord."

Here we pray for the *Lords of the Council,* the chief advisers of the Queen, and the *Nobility* or Peers of the realm. We ask for them *grace, wisdom, and understanding,* for they need these blessings in their high station, and God alone gives them. He gives grace— "The Lord will give grace and glory." (*Psalm* lxxxiv. 11.) He gives wisdom and understanding—"For the Lord giveth wisdom; out of His mouth cometh knowledge and understanding." (*Prov.* ii. 6. See also *St. James*, i. 5. 1 *Kings*, iii. 12.)

We pray also for the *magistrates* of the land, for those who are put in authority under the Queen, that they may *execute justice*, and *maintain* or uphold *the truth.* In David's old age he said, "He that ruleth over men must be just, ruling in the fear of. God." (2 *Sam.* xxiii. 3.) And in other countries where the magistrates are not upright and just, the people are in a miserable condition. When the judges of Israel afflicted the just, and took bribes, and turned aside the poor from their right, God's prophet said it was an evil time. (*Amos*, v. 12, 13.) So we may well pray for our judges and magistrates, "that they may judge not for man but for the Lord," and that "the fear of the Lord may be upon them." (2 *Chron.* xix. 6, 7. See also *Ezra*, vii. 25, 26.)

"That it may please Thee to bless and keep all Thy people :
 "We beseech Thee to hear us, good Lord."

It has been thought that as we have just been praying for the rulers of this land, we go on in this petition to pray for those whom they rule. But the words are too wide to be thus restricted, and the better explanation is this. We prayed before for Christ's Church as one body; here we pray for His people separately, as the many members which compose it. They are scattered up and down through the world, but He knows them all— "The Lord knoweth them that are His." (2 *Tim.* ii. 19.) "I am the Good Shepherd," said our blessed Lord, "and know My sheep." (*St. John*, x. 14.) We ask *blessing* from Him who was sent to bless us—"God having raised up His Son Jesus, sent Him to bless you." (*Acts*, iii. 26.) We ask safe *keeping* at His hands Who is "able to keep us from falling." (*Jude, v.* 24.)

"That it may please Thee to give to all nations, unity, peace, and concord :
 " We beseech Thee to hear us, good Lord."

This petition extends to the whole world, and embraces every nation of which it is composed; for "God hath made of one blood all nations of men for to dwell on all the face of the earth," (*Acts*, xvii. 26.) and therefore all have a claim on our prayers. And what do we ask for them? *Unity* at home—"Behold, how good and joyful a thing it is, brethren, to dwell together in unity!" (*Psalm* cxxxiii. 1.) and *peace* and *concord* with one another—"The Lord will give His people the blessing of peace." (*Psalm* xxix. 10.) Peace is so great a blessing, that the captive Jews were bidden to pray even that their conquerors, the Babylonians, might enjoy it—"Seek the peace of the city whither I have caused you to be carried away captives, and pray unto the Lord for it; for in the peace thereof shall ye have peace." (*Jer.* xxix. 7.) When we offer up this petition, we should remember the American nation, recently divided and torn by a fierce and bloody war, and should pray that Micah's prophecy may be fulfilled in this day—"They shall beat their swords into ploughshares, and their spears into pruning hooks; nation shall not lift up a sword against nation, neither shall they learn war any more; but they shall sit every man under his vine and under his fig tree, and none shall make them afraid." (*Micah*, iv. 3, 4.)

"That it may please Thee to give us a heart to love and dread Thee, and diligently to live after Thy commandments:

"We beseech Thee to hear us, good Lord."

Here we turn back from the world to the Church, and ask for ourselves and our fellow Christians, a *heart* to *love* and dread, *i. e.* fear, God. The heart, in man, is the source of all thought, will, and action. What the heart is, the whole man is; therefore God says—"Give me thy heart;" (*Prov.* xxiii. 26.) and we should answer with David—"O God, my heart is ready, my heart is ready!" (*Psalm* cviii. 1.) Two motives should rule our hearts; the love of God, and the fear of God. The love of God draws us to do what is right—"For this is the love of God, that we keep His Commandments." (1 *John*, v. 3.) The fear of God makes us avoid what is wrong—"The fear of the Lord is to hate evil." (*Prov.* viii. 13.) We need both these principles of action. Therefore St. Paul prayed for the Thessalonians, "The Lord direct your hearts into the love of God;" (2 *Thess.* iii. 5.) and exhorted the Hebrews to "serve God acceptably with reverence and godly fear." (*Heb.* xii. 28.) But love is the more excellent principle of the two; for "the fear of the Lord is the beginning of wisdom;" (*Psalm* cxi. 10.) but "love is the fulfilling of the Law." (*Rom.* xiii. 10.)

If our hearts are filled with the fear and love of God, we shall *diligently live* after His *Commandments.* "This is love, that we walk after His Commandments." (2 *St. John, v.* 6.) "That thou mightest fear the Lord thy God, to keep all His statutes and commandments." (*Deut.* vi. 2.)

"That it may please Thee to give to all Thy people increase of grace, to hear meekly Thy Word, and to receive it with pure affection, and to bring forth the fruits of the Spirit :
"We beseech Thee to hear us, good Lord."

By *grace* we mean the inward help which God for the sake of Jesus Christ bestows upon fallen man, by the Holy Ghost, that he may attain everlasting life. Grace comes from God—"The Lord will give grace and glory." (*Psalm* lxxxiv. 11.) It comes through Jesus Christ—"Grace and truth came by Jesus Christ." (*St. John*, i. 17. See also *Rom.* v. 15.) Without it man can do nothing ; but with it he is exhorted to work out his salvation—"Work out your own salvation with fear and trembling, for it is God which worketh in you, both to will and to do of His good pleasure." (*Phil.* ii. 12, 13. See also 2 *Cor.* iii. 5.) We pray that God's people may have an *increase of grace ;* for although grace has been already given them, first in Baptism, and since in other Christian ordinances, they need a constant supply of it—"And of His fulness

have all we received, and grace for grace." (*St. John*, i.
16.) "God is able to make all grace abound toward
you." (2 *Cor.* ix. 8.) We ask for grace, 1. To *hear
God's Word meekly*, as St. James exhorts us to do.
" Receive with meekness the engrafted Word, which is
able to save your souls." (*St. James*, i. 21. See also
1 *Thess.* ii. 13.) 2. To *receive it with pure affection ;* as
did the Psalmist, who could say, " Lord, what love have
I unto Thy Law ; all the day long is my study in it ;"
and " Consider, O Lord, how I love Thy commandments." (*Psalm* cxix. 97, 159.) 3. *To bring forth the
fruits of the Spirit.* What are these fruits ? "The fruit
of the Spirit is love, joy, peace, long-suffering, gentle-
ness, goodness, faith, meekness, temperance." (*Gal.* v.
22, 23.) " The fruit of the Spirit is in all goodness and
righteousness and truth." (*Eph.* v. 9.) Such are the
fruits or effects which God's Word should produce in
our hearts; but then we must hide it there—"Thy
words have I hid within my heart, that I should not
sin against Thee ;" (*Psalm* cxix. 11.) we must store
it there—" Therefore shall ye lay up these My words
in your heart, and in your soul ;" (*Deut.* xi. 18.) for only
then will the good seed bring forth fruit to perfection.

"That it may please Thee to bring into the way of
truth all such as have erred, and are deceived :
"We beseech Thee to hear us, good Lord."

The *Way of Truth* is the narrow way "which leadeth
unto life ;" (*St. Matt.* vii. 14.) " the path of the just,"
which "is as the shining light, that shineth more and
more unto the perfect day." (*Prov.* iv. 18.)
In old times a Christian was called a traveller, because he was journeying on that path; and Heaven was
called his home, his country, his fatherland. But the
way is narrow, steep, and rugged, and beset with
dangers. Our Lord Himself says, " Few there be that
find it." (*St. Matt.* vii. 14.) It is no marvel that many go
astray ; and for such wanderers we pray, whether they
have erred through their own wilfulness, negligence,
or ignorance, or have been led astray by others. Thus

Abraham prayed for wicked Sodom : (*Gen.* xviii. 23–33.)
Samuel for the Israelites : (1 *Sam.* xii. 23.) and Job for
his friends who had displeased God : (*Job*, xlii. 8.) and
St. John says, "If any man see his brother sin a sin
which is not unto death, he shall ask, and He shall give
him life for them that sin not unto death." (1 *St. John*,
v. 16.)

"That it may please Thee to strengthen such as do
stand; and to comfort and help the weak-hearted; and
to raise up them that fall; and finally to beat down
Satan under our feet:
"We beseech Thee to hear us, good Lord."

The life of the Christian is a state of warfare. He is
called on to "fight the good fight of faith : (1 *Tim.*
vi. 12.) to "war a good warfare." (1 *Tim.* i. 18.)
"Watch ye," says St. Paul, "stand fast in the faith,
quit you like men, be strong." (1 *Cor.* xvi. 13.) And
in this petition we pray for the good soldiers of Jesus
Christ. (2 *Tim.* ii. 3.) These are in three classes ; 1.
Such as do stand ; 2. *The weak-hearted* ; 3. *Them that
fall.*
1. Them that stand are such Christians as St. Paul
calls "strong :" (*Rom.* xv. 1.) "strong in the Lord, and
in the power of His might." (*Eph.* vi. 10.) Either they
have been kept by God's grace in the state of salvation
wherein they were placed at their baptism, or they have
been restored to it by God's mercy through Christ
Jesus, on their true repentance. For these we pray
that God would grant them "to be strengthened with
might by His Spirit in the inner man." (*Eph.* iii. 16.)
2. The weak-hearted are Christians of a naturally
low and feeble character, or whose courage has been
shaken by past sin, and who are over fearful as to their
spiritual state. Such persons are deficient in faith and
hope, and they are very likely in consequence to become
slothful, and give up the struggle on account of its
difficulties. We pray God to *comfort* these persons, for
they are sad; to *help* them, for they are weak; and we

3

know that He will fulfil our prayer, for "a bruised reed shall He not break, and the smoking flax shall He not quench." (*Isa.* xlii. 3. See also *Psalm* cxlvii. 3.)

3. Them that fall, are Christians who by wilful sin have dropped out of their former state of grace. We pray to God for them, for He alone can raise them up—"He lifteth up those that fall;" (*Psalm* cxlv. 14.) "The Lord helpeth them that are fallen." (*Psalm* cxlvi. 8.) And in His strength the Christian soldier may say, "Rejoice not against me, O mine enemy; when I fall, I shall arise." (*Micah*, vii. 8.)

And since in this conflict *Satan* is our great adversary, we beseech God, finally, when the warfare is accomplished, to beat him down under our feet. The old prophecy has been fulfilled; (*Gen.* iii. 5.) Christ has bruised the serpent's head. We pray that the New Testament promise may be fulfilled too—"The God of peace shall bruise Satan under your feet shortly;" (*Rom.* xvi. 20.) and that with the Captain of our Salvation we may "go upon the lion and the adder," and tread "the young lion and the dragon" under our feet. (*Psalm* xci. 13.)

"That it may please Thee to succour, help, and comfort, all that are in danger, necessity, and tribulation:

"We beseech Thee to hear us, good Lord."

As this world is full of sin, so is it full of suffering; and the suffering is the natural consequence or fruit of the sin. But our Lord Jesus Christ, who "bare our sins in His own body on the tree," (1 *St. Peter*, ii. 24.) has also "borne our griefs, and carried our sorrows." (*Isaiah*, liii. 4.) And therefore, "in that He Himself hath suffered being tempted, He is able to succour them that are tempted." (*Heb.* ii. 18.) His heart is full of pity for sufferers, whether in danger either of body or soul, in want, or in trouble of any kind. He "comforteth us in all our tribulation;" (2 *Cor.* i. 4.) "He shall deliver the poor when he crieth; the needy also, and him that hath no helper." (*Psalm* lxxii. 12. See also *Deut.* iv. 30, 31; *St. Matt.* xi. 28.)

"That it may please Thee to preserve all that travel by land or by water, all women labouring of child, all sick persons, and young children; and to show Thy pity upon all prisoners and captives:

"We beseech Thee to hear us, good Lord."

In this petition we invoke God's protecting care over those who, for different reasons, stand in special need of it.

1. We pray for *travellers*. In old times these were exposed to danger; *by land*, from bad roads, highway-robbers, and want of human help in lonely places; *by water*, from the unskilfulness of sailors, and the want of the mariner's compass. These dangers no longer exist, but yet fearful accidents do still happen; and when we travel, it is only by the goodness of God that we are preserved from them. And God has promised to protect His people in their journeys—"The Lord shall preserve thy going out and thy coming in, from this time forth, and even for evermore." (*Psalm* cxxi. 8. See also *Psalm* cvii. 23–30.)

2. For *women labouring of child*, since they are bearing directly the punishment laid upon Eve, our common mother, at the Fall—"In sorrow thou shalt bring forth children." (*Gen.* iii. 16.)

3. For *sick persons*, for they are undergoing a chastisement from the hand of God—"I kill and I make alive; I wound, and I heal: neither is there any that can deliver out of My hand." (*Deut.* xxxii. 39.) Often it is a direct punishment for sin; as in the case of the Israelites, (*Lev.* xxvi. 14–17.) of King Jehoram, (2 *Chron.* xxi. 12–15.) and of certain Corinthians, (1 *Cor.* xi. 30.) But it is said of our Lord Jesus, "Himself took our infirmities, and bare our sicknesses;" (*St. Matt.* viii. 17.) and we commend all sick persons to Him, in the assurance that He will heal them, or if He sees it better for them still to suffer, will comfort them—"The Lord comfort him when he lieth sick upon his bed; make Thou all his bed in his sickness." (*Psalm* xli. 3.)

4. For *young children*. These need our prayers, because they are so weak and helpless, and also because they are unable to pray for themselves. We know that our prayers for them will be heard, for our Saviour loves little children, as He showed on earth by taking them up in His arms, putting His hands on them, and blessing them. (*St. Mark*, x. 16.)

5. For *prisoners and captives*. These are either prisoners of war, persons imprisoned for debt, or criminals. The condition of all is sad, and they need our sympathy. Hence, they are among those sufferers who represent to us our Lord Himself. At the Last Day He will say to those on His right hand, "I was in prison, and ye came unto Me." (*St. Matt.* xxv. 36.) And if we are not able ourselves to visit prisoners, we must show our charity by praying for them, bearing in mind St. Paul's exhortation, "Remember them that are in bonds, as bound with them." (*Heb.* xiii. 8. See also *Psalm* lxxix. 11.)

"That it may please Thee to defend, and provide for, the fatherless children, and widows, and all that are desolate and oppressed:

"We beseech Thee to hear us, good Lord."

Fatherless children and widows, having lost their earthly supporter and guide, are, at best, in a sad and bereaved condition. And so God takes them under His special protection—"He is a Father of the fatherless, and defendeth the cause of the widow." (*Psalm* lxviii. 5. See also *Deut.* x. 18; *Psalm* cxlvi. 9; *Jer.* xlix. 11.) We may therefore come to Him boldly, and plead their cause, and that of all who are desolate and oppressed. The *desolate* are persons without friends or helpers; the *oppressed*, those who are suffering evil at the hands of others. "Many are the afflictions of the righteous, but the Lord delivereth him out of them all." (*Psalm* xxxiv. 17. See also *Isaiah* lxiii. 9.)

"That it may please Thee to have mercy upon all men:

"We beseech Thee to hear us, good Lord."

We are taught that God, our Saviour, "will have all men to be saved, and to come to the knowledge of the truth;" (1 *Tim.* ii. 4.) that "He was the true Light, which lighteth every man that cometh into the world." (*St. John,* i. 9.) Therefore, as St. Paul exhorts us, (1 *Tim.* ii. 1.) we should pray for *all men;* and the more we pray, the more we shall learn the value of the souls for whom Christ died.

"That it may please Thee to forgive our enemies, persecutors, and slanderers, and to turn their hearts:
"We beseech Thee to hear us, good Lord."

Our *enemies* are those who hate us; and these are of two sorts—*persecutors,* who would do us harm by deeds, and *slanderers,* who would do us harm by words. All these we must not only ourselves forgive, but ask God to forgive them also. It is a hard matter for human nature to do this. The very best among heathens knew nothing of such a spirit of love; neither did the Jews, even in our Lord's time. They said with them of old time, "Thou shalt love thy neighbour, and hate thine enemy." (*St. Matt.* v. 43.) But members of Christ should act as did their Head. He prayed on the Cross for His persecutors, "Father, forgive them, for they know not what they do:" (*St. Luke,* xxiii. 34.) and He bids us do the same, "Pray for them which despitefully use you, and persecute you." (*St. Matt.* v. 44.) After His Example, St. Stephen prayed for his murderers; (*Acts,* vii. 60.) and St. Paul says of himself and his fellow Apostles, "Being defamed, we intreat." (1 *Cor.* iv. 13.)

"That it may please Thee to give and preserve to our use the kindly fruits of the earth, so as in due time we may enjoy them:
"We beseech Thee to hear us, good Lord."

The *kindly fruits of the earth* mean its natural fruits; those which, according to its kind, it brings forth in the order of God's Providence. We ask for refreshing

showers and warm sunshine to ripen the crops, and for
fine weather in which to gather and store them up; for
all these come directly from God's Hand. "He bring-
eth forth grass for the cattle, and green herb for the
service of men; that He may bring food out of the earth."
(*Psalm* civ. 14, 15. See also *Deut.* xi. 13–15; *Psalm*
lxv. 9–13; *Acts*, xiv. 17.) This petition is an enlarge-
ment of those words in our Lord's own Prayer, "Give
us this day our daily bread," in their simplest and most
literal sense; and if we remember what a difference a
good or a bad harvest makes to all, especially to the
poor, we shall join in it heartily.

"That it may please Thee to give us true repentance;
to forgive us all our sins, negligences, and ignorances;
and to endue us with the grace of Thy Holy Spirit to
amend our lives according to Thy Holy Word:
   "We beseech Thee to hear us, good Lord."

At the close of our intercessions we pray (1) for *true
repentance.* Without this we cannot expect to be heard;
for God says of the impenitent, "When ye spread forth
your hands, I will hide mine eyes from you." (*Isaiah*, i.
15. See also *Jer.* xiv. 12; *Ezekiel*, viii. 18.) It is
only by true repentance that sinners can hope to be
saved—"Godly sorrow worketh repentance unto salvation, not to be repented of;" (2 *Cor.* vii. 10.) and to
it God has attached the forgiveness of sins—"Him hath
God exalted with His right hand, to be a Prince and
a Saviour, for to give repentance unto Israel, and
forgiveness of sins." (*Acts*, v. 31.) There is a false
repentance like that of Ahab, (1 *Kings*, xxi. 27.) and
of Judas; (*St. Matt.* xxvii. 3–5.) but this avails
nothing—"The sorrow of the world worketh death."
(2 *Cor.* vii. 10.) True repentance has its root in
humility, like that of the Publican; (*St. Luke*, xviii. 13.)
is thorough and earnest, like that of the Corinthians;
(2 *Cor.* vii. 11.) and proceeds from love of God. (2.)
We pray for forgiveness of our *sins*, or acts committed
contrary to God's Law; these are the "things which
we ought not to have done:" (*Gen. Confession.*) of our

negligences, or omission of services we should have rendered to God; these are the things "left undone" which "we ought to have done:" (*Gen. Confession.*) of our *ignorances*, or things which we had the opportunity of knowing, but do not know because we have neglected to learn them. In these several ways we have all, more or less, offended God—"All have sinned, and come short of the glory of God;" (*Rom.* iii. 23.) but "with the Lord there is mercy, and with Him there is plenteous. redemption." (*Psalm* cxxx. 7. See also *Psalm* xxxii. 5.) We pray for *the grace of God's Holy Spirit, to amend our lives.* There can be no real amendment without the Holy Spirit of God. Any attempt to amend, except under His influence, is only sweeping and garnishing the heart for the unclean spirit to return with seven other spirits more wicked than himself. (*St. Luke,* xi. 24–26.) But if we "walk in the Spirit," we "shall not fulfil the lusts of the flesh;" (*Gal.* v. 16.) and the promise of God stands sure, "I will put My Spirit within you, and cause you to walk in My statutes." (*Ezekiel,* xxxvi. 27.) Lastly, we pray God. for grace to amend our lives *according to His Holy Word,* because that is the only standard which may be trusted. The world is false and imperfect, and we cannot judge ourselves truly by its corrupt changing rules; but "the law is holy, and the commandment holy and just and good." (*Rom.* vii. 12. See also *Psalm* xix. 7–11.)

"Son of God, we beseech Thee to hear us.

"Son of God, we beseech Thee to hear us.

"O Lamb of God, that takest away the sins of the world:

"Grant us Thy peace.

"O Lamb of God, that takest away the sins of the world:

"Have mercy upon us.

"O Christ, hear us.

"O Christ, hear us.

We close our Intercessions with an earnest appeal to

our Lord Jesus. (1.) As the Son of God. This He confessed Himself to be when the question was solemnly put by the High Priest, "Art Thou the Christ, the Son of the Blessed? And Jesus said, I am." (*St. Mark*, xiv. 61, 62.) (2.) As the Lamb of God—"For He is the very Paschal Lamb, which was offered for us, and hath taken away the sin of the world." (*Pref. for Easter Day in Com. Office.*) Every sacrifice offered to God, from the time when righteous Abel "brought of the firstlings of his flock," (*Gen.* iv. 4.) was a type of Him; but most of all the Paschal Lamb, which prefigured in the closest manner His atoning sacrifice. Therefore, when St. John the Baptist began his office of preparing the way for the Lord, he proclaimed, "Behold the Lamb of God, which taketh away the sin of the world." (*St. John*, i. 29.) St. Peter reminds his disciples that they were redeemed "with the Precious Blood of Christ, as of a lamb without blemish and without spot." (1 *St. Peter*, i. 19.) "He bare our sins in His own Body on the tree." (1 *St. Peter*, ii. 24.) Yet, although "by one offering He hath perfected for ever them that are sanctified," (*Heb.* x. 14.) we pray, "O Lamb of God, that *takest* away the sins of the world." And this because He is ever pleading His Passion before the Father—ever pleading for us through it. His sacrifice for sins was "for ever." (*Heb.* x. 12.) Even on His Father's throne He bears the semblance of "a Lamb as it had been slain;" (*Rev.* v. 6.) and the angels praise Him, saying, "Worthy is the Lamb that was slain, to receive power, and riches, and wisdom, and strength, and honour, and glory, and blessing." (*Rev.* v. 12.) (3.) As the Christ, the Anointed One, or Messiah, of whom Daniel prophesied, "After threescore and two weeks shall Messiah be cut off, but not for Himself." (*Dan.* ix. 26.) Our Lord Jesus was anointed, not with oil like earthly kings and priests, but with the Holy Ghost, Who descended upon Him at His baptism, fulfilling Isaiah's prophecy—"The Spirit of the Lord God is upon Me; because the Lord hath anointed Me to preach good tidings unto the meek," (*Isaiah*, lxi. 1.)

applied by our Lord to Himself. (*St. Luke*, iv. 18–21.)
St. Andrew, the first disciple, bore witness, "We have
found the Messias, which is, being interpreted, the
Christ." (*St. John*, i. 41.) And St. Peter to Cornelius,
"How God anointed Jesus of Nazareth with the Holy
Ghost, and with power." (*Acts*, x. 38.)

By these three titles we call upon our Saviour,
beseeching Him (1) to hear us. It is much if He does
this after our past neglect of Him; and therefore His
people have ever entreated earnestly for a hearing.
Thus Job prayed, "Hear, I beseech Thee;" (*Job*, xlii.
4.) and David, "Unto Thee will I cry, O Lord my
strength; think no scorn of me; lest, if Thou make as
though Thou hearest not, I become like them that go
down into the pit;" (*Psalm* xxviii. 1.) and Elijah,
"Hear me, O Lord, hear me." (1 *Kings*, xviii. 37.)
(2.) To grant us His peace, *i. e.* peace with God. We
ask this of our Lord Jesus, "for He is our peace."
(*Eph.* ii. 14.) "Having abolished in His flesh the
enmity, even the law of commandments contained in
ordinances; for to make in Himself of twain one new
man, so making peace." (*Eph.* ii. 15.) Thus, "being
justified by faith, we have peace with God;" (*Rom.* v.
1.) from which flows peace in ourselves—"Great is the
peace that they have who love Thy law;" (*Psalm* cxix.
165.) and with our fellow-men—"When a man's ways
please the Lord, he maketh even his enemies to be at
peace with him." (*Prov.* xvi. 7.) (3.) To have mercy
upon us—the cry which has arisen from penitent hearts
since David prayed, "Have mercy upon me, O Lord."
(*Psalm* li. 1. See also *Zech.* i. 12.)

IV. THE SUPPLICATIONS.

THE old Litanies ended with the Intercessions; but
about the seventh century the Lord's Prayer was added,
because no Office was thought complete without it, and
supplications for aid and deliverance on account of the

miseries the Roman empire was then enduring from
the invasion of barbarian nations. These supplications
are most suitable in times of public distress or persecution; but they are never out of place, since suffering is
the very proof that we are God's children. (*Heb.* xii. 7,
8.) "All that will live godly in Christ Jesus shall
suffer persecution;" (2 *Tim.* iii. 12.) and as time passes,
such prayers become more and more suitable, since the
Church is warned of troublous times in the last days.
(*verse* 1.) They are therefore added to our Litany.

"Lord, have mercy upon us.
"Christ, have mercy upon us.
"Lord, have mercy upon us."

Fallen man cannot too often cry to God for mercy.
Here the petition is made to the Three Persons of the
Trinity, and in this manner it has been offered up from
the earliest ages of the Church, the priest and the people
uttering it by turns.

"Our Father, which art in Heaven, hallowed be Thy
Name. Thy kingdom come. Thy Will be done in
earth, as it is in Heaven. Give us this day our daily
bread. And forgive us our trespasses, as we forgive
them that trespass against us. And lead us not into
temptation; but deliver us from evil. Amen."

This is the very prayer which our Lord gave us,
and commanded us to use—"When ye pray, say Our
Father," &c. (*St. Luke*, xi. 2.) From the earliest days,
therefore, the Church has used it in all her Services.
Tertullian says that we begin with it, because it is the
foundation upon which all other prayers should be
built; and St. Augustine, that we close with it, because
it is the perfection of all prayer. Accordingly, every
one of our Offices contains the Lord's Prayer. Our
present form of prayer consists of several Offices, distinct
and perfect in themselves, though now commonly used
together. Hence it is that the Lord's Prayer is so often
repeated. The Lord's Prayer consists of an introduction
and seven petitions.

Introduction. "*Our Father, which art in Heaven.*" Even God's ancient people were allowed to pray to Him as their Father—"Thou, O Lord, art our Father; we are the clay, and Thou art the potter; and we are all the work of Thy hand." (*Isaiah,* lxiv. 8. See also 1 *Chron.* xxix. 10.) Much more may we thus pray, who "have received the spirit of adoption, whereby we cry, Abba, Father!" (*Rom.* viii. 15. See also 1 *St. John,* iii. 1.) We say *which art in Heaven,* for it is from thence that He has promised to hear us—"If My people, which are called by My Name, shall humble themselves, and pray, and seek My face, and turn from their wicked ways, then will I hear from Heaven." (2 *Chron.* vii. 14.) Therefore, "let us lift up our heart with our hands unto God in the heavens." (*Lam.* iii. 41.)

Petition I. *Hallowed be Thy Name.* We pray here that God's Name may be regarded as holy; may be known, worthily praised, honoured, and adored, by all the works of His hands. We poor creatures can add nothing to the holiness of God's Name; still He accounts that we hallow It when we praise and adore It. Thus David exclaims, "Give the Lord the honour due unto His Name; worship the Lord with holy worship." (*Psalm* xxix. 2. See also *Psalm* xcvi. 7, 8.) We also pray that God's great Name may be sanctified in us and other Christians; for as It is blasphemed through the unholy lives of any who are called by It, (*Rom.* ii. 24.) so is It glorified by their holiness—"Let your light so shine before men, that they may see your good works, and glorify your Father which is in Heaven." (*St. Matt.* v. 16.)

Petition II. *Thy kingdom come.* This petition is thus enlarged in the Burial Service—"That it may please Thee, of Thy gracious goodness, shortly to accomplish the number of Thine elect, and to hasten Thy kingdom." This is the constant prayer of the Church, and of the Spirit who dwells in her—"The Spirit and the Bride say, Come." (*Rev.* xxii. 20.) For this coming of their Lord Christians look—"Our conversation is in Heaven,' from whence also we look for the Saviour, the Lord Jesus Christ :" (*Phil.* iii. 20. See also *Titus*, ii. 13.) for it they wait—"Waiting for the coming of our Lord Jesus Christ:" (1 *Cor.* i. 7. See also 1 *Thess.* i. 10.) and for it they should be ready —"Be ye therefore ready also; for the Son of man cometh at an hour when ye think not." (*St. Luke*, xii. 40.)

Petition III. *Thy Will be done on earth, as it is in Heaven.* We pray here that God's Will may be fulfilled *in* us, and *by* us. 1. *In us*, through our submission to what His Providence ordains for us; after the example of the Lord Jesus, who prayed, "Not My will, but Thine, be done." (*St. Luke*, xxii. 42.) Thus Eli said in affliction, "It is the Lord, let Him do what seemeth Him good;" (1 *Sam.* iii. 18.) and David, "Behold, here am I, let Him do to me as seemeth good;" (2 *Sam.* xv. 26.) and the Christians of Cæsarea, "The Will of the Lord be done." (*Acts*, xxi. 14.) 2. *By us*, through our fashioning our lives according to His Commandments—"For this is the Will of God, even your sanctification." (1 *Thess.* iv. 3. See also *Rom.* xii. 1.) We know that the angels fulfil God's Will perfectly— "O praise the Lord, ye angels of His, ... ye that fulfil His commandment, and hearken unto the voice of His words. O praise the Lord, all ye His hosts; ye servants of His that do His pleasure ;" (*Psalm* ciii. 20, 21.) and we pray that we and our fellow Christians may do the same, as far as our nature allows it.

These three petitions relate chiefly to the glory of God; the four which follow relate to the wants of men.

Petition IV. *Give us this day our daily bread.* Man has a two-fold nature, body and soul; and the wants of each part are brought before God in this petition. We ask Him "to give us all things that be needful, both for our souls and bodies." (*Church Catechism.*) Daily bread for the body means all that is necessary for its welfare. For this Jacob prayed—"If God will be with me, and will keep me in this way that I go, and will give me bread to eat and raiment to put on."

(*Gen.* xxviii. 20.) And Agur—"Feed me with food convenient for me." (*Prov.* xxx. 8.) Daily bread for the soul means such spiritual help as the soul needs day by day; it means the grace of God given through prayer, by reading of the Scripture and holy teaching; and, chief of all, it means Christ Himself in the Holy Communion—for He said, "Labour not for the meat which perisheth, but for that meat which endureth unto eternal life, which the Son of man shall give unto you;" (*St. John*, vi. 27.) and "I am the Bread of Life." (*St. John*, vi. 35.)

Petition V. *And forgive us our trespasses, as we forgive them that trespass against us.* On the Mount of Beatitudes, Christ, the Lawgiver of the New Dispensation, laid down this law : "With what measure ye mete it shall be measured to you again." (*St. Matt.* vii. 2.) And here He carries it into His Prayer, showing that only in proportion to the forgiveness we grant can we be forgiven. To fix this principle the more firmly in our hearts and minds, our Lord adds a commentary to this clause of the Lord's Prayer, and this one alone—"For if ye forgive men their trespasses, your Heavenly Father will also forgive you; but if ye forgive not men their trespasses, neither will your Father forgive your trespasses." (*St. Matt.* vi. 14, 15.) He also delivered a parable on the subject, that of the unmerciful servant. (*St. Matt.* xviii. 23–85.)

The closer we look into our own hearts, the more we shall see our daily need of forgiveness. But there is no hope of our receiving it unless we love our enemies, and freely pardon them. Let us therefore be "kind one to another, tender-hearted, forgiving one another, even as God, for Christ's sake, hath forgiven" us; (*Eph.* iv. 32.) and we shall experience, that the Lord is "merciful and gracious, long-suffering, and abundant in goodness and truth; keeping mercy for thousands, forgiving iniquity and transgression and sin." (*Exodus*, xxxiv. 6, 7.)

Petition VI. *And lead us not into temptation.* Temptation means trial, whether by a friend or an enemy;

and if we never meet it we shall never know what we really are, or learn dependence on God. Thus God tried the Children of Israel—"Thou shalt remember all the way which the Lord thy God led thee these forty years in the wilderness, to humble thee, and to prove thee, and to know what was in thine heart." (*Deut.* viii. 2.) Thus He tried the faith of Abraham, (*Gen.* xxii.) and the patience of Job. (*Job*, i., ii.) Of such trials St. James says, "Count it all joy when ye fall into divers temptations," and "Blessed is the man that endureth temptation; for when he is tried he shall receive the crown of life." (*St. James*, i. 2, 12.) But we are very weak, and therefore we pray not to be led into temptation beyond our strength. Thus our Lord warned His disciples: "Pray that ye enter not into temptation." (*St. Luke*, xxii. 40.) And we may trust the assurance—"God is faithful, who will not suffer you to be tempted above that ye are able." (1 *Cor.* x. 13.)

There is another sort of temptation, which is altogether the work of the devil. This consists in seducing or enticing to sin. Thus the devil tempted Eve—"The serpent beguiled Eve through his subtlety." (2 *Cor.* xi. 3.) In this sense, "God tempteth no man;" (*James*, i. 13.) and we pray Him to keep us from all such temptations.

Petition VII. *But deliver us from evil. Amen.* Evil here means everything that is adverse to us, and chiefly "the Evil One, Satan;" who is the source and fountain of evil—"The devil sinneth from the beginning." (1 *St. John*, iii. 8.) "When he speaketh a lie, he speaketh of his own." (*St. John*, viii. 44.) The world too is evil. St. Paul calls it, "this present evil world;" (*Gal.* i. 4.) and our Lord prayed on the eve of His Crucifixion, that we might be delivered from the evil of it—"I pray not that Thou shouldest take them out of the world, but that Thou shouldest keep them from the evil." (*St. John*, xvii. 15.) And man's heart is evil—"The imagination of man's heart is evil from his youth." (*Gen.* viii. 21.) From the devil, the world, and flesh, we ask deliverance.

We also pray to be delivered from the evils of this life, such as sickness, poverty, and loss of friends; but we must do this in perfect submission to God's Will, knowing that they are not really evils to us if God appoints them for us—that "all things work together for good to them that love God;" (*Rom.* viii. 28.) and that "if God be for us, who can be against us?" (*verse* 31.)

Amen, is an ancient Hebrew word, often used by our Lord, and translated "Verily" in His discourses, (*St. John*, v. 24. and elsewhere.) When used after a prayer it means that we consent to it, and join in it. St. Jerome calls it the seal of prayer. It was the appointed response in Jewish worship—"Blessed be the Lord God of Israel, for ever and ever. And all the people said Amen." (1 *Chron.* xvi. 36.) Its use has been continued in the Christian Church. St. Paul speaks of Christians saying Amen at the giving of thanks. (1 *Cor.* xiv. 16.) And it is uttered by the heavenly host in their praises of God—"Amen: Blessing, and glory, and wisdom, and thanksgiving, and honour, and power, and might, be unto our God for ever and ever. Amen." (*Rev.* vii. 12.)

"O Lord, deal not with us after our sins:
"Neither reward us after our iniquities."

King David said of God, "He hath not dealt with us after our sins, nor rewarded us according to our wickednesses; (*Psalm* ciii. 10.) and his words are here turned into a prayer. *After* here means according to. If we are dealt with according to our sins, we must be punished, for punishment is the due reward of sin. This the dying thief confessed upon the cross, "We indeed justly, for we receive the due reward of our deeds." (*St. Luke*, xxiii. 41.) See also *Rom.* vi. 23. Sin, according to God's dispensations, finds out the sinner, and overtakes him in the form of punishment. But with God is forgiveness—"There is forgiveness with Thee." (*Psalm* cxxx. 4.)

"Let us pray.
"O God, merciful Father, that despisest not the

sighing of a contrite heart, nor the desire of such as be sorrowful; mercifully assist our prayers that we make before Thee in all our troubles and adversities whensoever they oppress us; and graciously hear us, that those evils which the craft and subtilty of the devil or man worketh against us, be brought to nought; and by the providence of Thy goodness they may be dispersed; that we Thy servants, being hurt by no persecutions, may evermore give thanks unto Thee in Thy holy Church; through Jesus Christ our Lord. Amen."

The minister says "Let us pray," to show that though he leaves for a time alternate prayer and speaks himself alone, yet the people must join with their hearts in what he utters.

The prayer which follows is from the ancient Sarum Office. The introduction contains an encouragement to pray, afforded by the gracious nature of God, and His pity for the afflicted—"He is gracious and merciful, slow to anger, and of great kindness." (*Joel*, ii. 13.) Then we ask (1) for God's help in the prayers we make in time of trouble, since of ourselves "we know not what we should pray for as we ought." (*Rom.* viii. 26.) (2) That God would bring to naught the devices of our enemies; so that they may not hurt us by any evil, or hinder us from serving Him. In the war which the devil is madly waging against the Most High, he uses much craft and subtlety—"Lest Satan should get an advantage of us, for we are not ignorant of his devices;" (2 *Cor.* ii. 11.) and his servants, the wicked, are like him—"The ungodly are froward even from their mother's womb; as soon as they are born they go astray and speak lies. They are as venomous as the poison of a serpent, even like the deaf adder that stoppeth her ears." (*Psalm* lviii. 3, 4.) See also *Psalm* xxxvii. 33. We offer up this, as all our other prayers, through Jesus Christ our Lord; for we have no claim to be heard but through Him. St. Gregory, a Father of the Church, says, "No man rightly calls upon God the Father but by the Son." Our Lord is the one

Mediator between God and man—"There is one God, and one Mediator between God and man, the man Christ Jesus;" (1 *Tim.* ii. 5.) and He said to His disciples, "Whatsoever ye shall ask the Father in My Name, He will give it you." (*St. John*, xvi. 23.)

"O Lord, arise, help us, and deliver us, for Thy Name's sake.

"O God, we have heard with our ears, and our fathers have declared unto us, the noble works that Thou didst in their days, and in the old time before them:

"O Lord, arise, help us, and deliver us, for Thine honour.

"Glory be to the Father, and to the Son, and to the Holy Ghost:

"As it was in the beginning, is now, and ever shall be, world without end. Amen."

These versicles and responses were formerly chanted at the beginning of the Litany, on the Second Rogation Day, in the Church of Salisbury. They are chiefly taken from *Psalm* xliv. "We have heard with our ears, O God, our fathers have told us, what Thou hast done in their time of old." (*verse* 1.) "Arise, and help us, and deliver us for Thy mercies' sake." (*verse* 26.) Thus Jacob pleaded with God His past mercies: "I am not worthy of the least of all the mercies, and of all the truth, which Thou hast shewed unto Thy servant; .... deliver me, I pray Thee, from the hand of my brother." (*Gen.* xxxii. 10, 11.) As did David: "Hear me when I call, O God of my righteousness; Thou hast set me at liberty when I was in trouble; have mercy upon me, and hearken unto my prayer;" (*Psalm* iv. 1.) and Nehemiah. (*Neh.* ix.) We ask God to *help* and *deliver* us for His *Name's sake*. In the same way Joshua pleaded for Israel; saying, "And what wilt Thou do unto Thy great Name?" (*Joshua*, vii. 9.) And the thought of past mercies leads us on to the Gloria Patri, though we say it on our knees as suits a penitential

4

office. The Gloria Patri is a very ancient doxology or
ascription of praise, which has been said in the Church
at least from the days of Clement of Alexandria, A. D.
190. It acknowledges the glory of the Three Persons
of the Trinity to be equal, and joins in the praise which
has been rendered to God from the beginning of time,
and will be rendered to Him "world without end," or
to all eternity.

"From our enemies defend us, O Christ:
  "Graciously look upon our afflictions.
"Pitifully behold the sorrows of our hearts:
  "Mercifully forgive the sins of Thy people.
"Favourably with mercy hear our prayers:
  "O Son of David, have mercy upon us.
"Both now and ever vouchsafe to hear us, O Christ:
  "Graciously hear us, O Christ; graciously hear us,
      O Lord Christ.
"O Lord, let Thy mercy be showed upon us:
  "As we do put our trust in Thee."

These are short earnest petitions for help and salvation, addressed to our Saviour Christ. The *enemies* from
whom we pray Him to *defend us*, are chiefly the enemies
of our souls, the world, the flesh, and the devil. We
ask Him to *look upon our afflictions*, and *behold* our
sorrows, because one glance of His eye will disperse
them at once. Thus the father of the possessed child
said, "I beseech Thee, look upon my son." (*St. Luke*, ix.
38.) The cry, "Son of David, have mercy upon me!"
prevailed with our Lord, when it was uttered by
blind Bartimeus; (*St. Mark*, x. 47, 48.) and the Syro-
Phœnician woman. (*St. Matt.* xv. 22.)

"Let us pray.
  "We humbly beseech Thee, O Father, mercifully to
look upon our infirmities; and for the glory of Thy
Name turn from us all those evils that we most
righteously have deserved; and grant, that in all our
troubles we may put our whole trust and confidence
in Thy mercy, and evermore serve Thee in holiness

and pureness of living, to Thy honour and glory; through our only Mediator and Advocate, Jesus Christ our Lord. Amen."

In this humble contrite prayer we bring before our Father's eye our infirmities, or weakness. Compare with it the Collect for the Fourth Sunday after Epiphany—"By reason of the frailty of our nature we cannot always stand upright;" and that for the First Sunday after Trinity—"through the weakness of our mortal nature we can do no good thing without Thee." Sin is the cause of weakness, as holiness is the cause of strength. Our infirmities are the fruit of the original sin which remains in us, although we are regenerate and made God's children by adoption and grace; and also of the sins which, alas! we daily fall into. The consciousness of sin made David say, "Have mercy upon me, O Lord, for I am weak." (*Psalm* vi. 2.) We go on to acknowledge that we have righteously deserved punishment. Thus Ezra said, "Thou, our God, hast punished us less than our iniquities deserve." (*Ezra*, ix. 13.) We pray that the evils we have deserved may be turned away; but, however this may be, intreat for trust and confidence in God's mercy. "Though He slay me," said Job, "yet will I trust in Him;" (*Job*, xiii. 15.) and St. Paul, in prison, and just before being brought to trial, said, "I know Whom I have believed, and am persuaded that He is able to keep that which I have committed unto Him against that day." (2 *Tim.* i. 12.) We pray finally for help to serve God aright, in the words of the Benedictus—"That He would give us; that we being delivered out of the hand of our enemies, might serve Him without fear." (*St. Luke*, i. 74.) And this for the honour and glory of God—"Not unto us, O Lord, not unto us, but unto Thy Name give the praise, for Thy loving mercy, and for Thy truth's sake." (*Psalm* cxv. 1.) See also *Isaiah*, xlviii. 9, 11.

"Let us pray:
"Almighty God, Who hast given us grace at this time with one accord to make our common supplications

unto Thee; and dost promise, that when two or three
are gathered together in Thy Name Thou wilt grant
their requests: Fulfil now, O Lord, the desires and
petitions of Thy servants, as may be most expedient for
them; granting us in this world knowledge of Thy truth,
and in the world to come life everlasting. Amen."

This concluding prayer is called the Prayer of St.
Chrysostom, Patriarch of Constantinople, A. D. 397, and
is taken from the Liturgy of the Eastern Church. It
acknowledges the goodness of our Lord Jesus, in
permitting us to make Him our common, that is, our
joint or united, supplications—and this *with one accord*
or consent, like strings in a musical instrument vi-
brating in harmony. Thus the early Christians "lifted
up their voice with one accord:" (*Acts*, iv. 24.) from
whence we gather that there was already a set form of
prayer in use among them, well known to all; even as
the forms of prayer in our Book of Common Prayer
ought to be well known to all Church people. Our
Lord has made us a special promise, "Where two or
three are gathered together in My Name, there am
I in the midst of them;" (*St. Matt.* xviii. 20.) and this
promise we plead. It was fulfilled in the case of the
early Christians. (*Acts*, iv. 31.) Ours too is the
promise made to Israel of old,—"In all places where I
record My Name I will come unto thee, and I will bless
thee." (*Exodus*, xx. 24.) Then, looking back on our
prayers, we ask our Lord to fulfil or grant our *desires*,
or unexpressed wishes; and our *petitions*, or wishes
expressed in words. Thus David, acknowledging God's
goodness in hearing him, says, "Thou hast given him
his heart's desire, and hast not denied him the request
of his lips." (*Psalm* xxi. 2.) But since "we know not
what we should pray for as we ought," (*Rom.* viii. 26.)
we leave it to our Lord to fulfil them as is most
expedient or fitting for us, lest, perchance, we should
"ask and receive not, because we ask amiss." (*St.
James*, iv. 3.) Only there are two things which we
may safely ask; the knowledge of God's truth here, and

everlasting life hereafter—"For this is good and acceptable in the sight of God our Saviour, Who will have all men to be saved, and to come to the knowledge of the truth;" (1 *Tim.* ii. 3, 4.) and He hath promised "to them, who by patient continuance in well-doing seek for glory and honour and immortality, eternal life." (*Rom.* ii. 7.)

"The grace of our Lord Jesus Christ, and the love of God, and the fellowship of the Holy Ghost, be with us all evermore. Amen."

This benedictory prayer, taken from 2 *Cor.* xiii. 14, closes the Litany. In it the minister commends himself and the people to the care of the ever-blessed Trinity, praying that we may partake of the *love* of God, Who Himself is love; (1 *St. John,* iv. 8.) of the *grace* of our Lord Jesus Christ, Who is "full of grace and truth;" (*St. John,* i. 14.) and of the *fellowship* or communion of the Holy Ghost, Who leads His people, (*Gal.* v. 18.) and dwells in them—"His Spirit, that dwelleth in you;" (*Rom.* viii. 11.) binding them together, and making them meet for the Presence of God among them—"In Whom ye also are builded together for an habitation of God through the Spirit." (*Eph.* ii. 22.)

QUESTIONS FOR EXAMINATION.

INTRODUCTION.

1. WHAT does the word Litany mean?
2. What sort of prayer do we now call a Litany?
3. How ancient are Litanies thought to be?
4. When do we hear of them in the Eastern Church?
5. When in the Western?
6. What was St. Gregory's Litany called, and why?
7. On what occasions were Litanies anciently said?
8. How did they come into more regular use?
9. When is the Litany of the English Church said?
10. What is the history of the Litany of our Church?
11. In what posture is it said, and for what reasons?
12. Into how many parts may it be divided?

I.—THE INVOCATIONS.

1. WHY do we begin the Litany with calling on God's Name?
2. Why is the First Person of the Trinity called God the Father?
3. Why do we say "of heaven?"
4. Who is the Second Person of the Trinity?
5. Why is He so addressed?
6. What is His incarnate Name?

7. Why do we say "Redeemer of the world?"
8. Who is the Third Person of the Trinity?
9. From Whom does He proceed?
10. By what Name do we call upon these Three Divine Persons in One?
11. What prayer is mingled with our Invocations?
12. What do we own ourselves to be?

II.—THE DEPRECATIONS.

1. To which Person of the blessed Trinity are the Deprecations addressed?
2. What do you mean by Deprecation?
3. What do we pray our Lord not to remember?
4. On what plea do we ask Him to spare us?
5. What may we take evil and mischief to mean here?
6. What is sin?
7. What are the two modes whereby the devil leads us to it?
8. What is the consequence of sin?
9. To what does the wrath of God bring sinners?
10. What causes blindness of heart? of what is it the punishment? and to what does it lead?
11. What is pride? Give an instance of it from Scripture.
12. What is vain-glory? Give an instance of it from Scripture.
13. What is hypocrisy? who did our Lord reprove for it?
14. What is envy? Give instances of it from Scripture.
15. What are hatred and malice?
16. Whence do envy, hatred, and malice, proceed?
17. What is meant by deadly sin?
18. Show how the world and the flesh and the devil are full of deceits.
19. How should we regard lightning and tempest?

20. What other judgments of God are named in the same petition?

21. Why do we pray against sudden death?

22. What is a Christian's duty towards the rulers of his country?

23. What are sedition, privy conspiracy, and rebellion?

24. What are false doctrine, heresy, and schism?

25. Show their sinfulness.

26. What is the cause of hardness of heart?

27. What brings the soul to contempt of God's Word and Commandment, and in what does it end?

28. Why are the actions of our Lord's life of infinite value?

29. Why do we plead the mystery of His Holy Incarnation? His Nativity? His Circumcision? His Baptism? His Fasting and Temptation? His Agony and Bloody Sweat? His Cross and Passion? His Death and Burial? His Resurrection? His Ascension? the Coming of the Holy Ghost?

30. Why do we ask for deliverance in time of tribulation? in time of wealth? in the hour of death? in the Day of Judgment?

III.—THE INTERCESSIONS.

1. WHAT is the meaning of intercession?

2. Explain the duty of intercessory prayer?

3. What encouragement have we to fulfil it?

4. What is our first intercession?

5. What is meant by God's holy Church universal?

6. Explain the duty of praying for the Queen?

7. What is the substance of the petitions for her?

8. On what grounds do we pray for the Prince of Wales?

9. What do we ask for the three orders of the Christian ministry?

10. What special claim have they on our prayers?

11. Why do we pray for the Lords of the Council, and all the Nobility?
12. What do we ask for them?
13. What is our prayer for the Magistrates of the land?
14. What is our prayer for all the people of God?
15. What do we ask for all nations?
16. What is unity?
17. Why do we pray for a *heart* to love and dread the Lord?
18. Do we need the motives both of fear and love?
19. How shall we live if we are ruled by both?
20. What is grace?
21. Why do we ask for an increase of grace?
22. To what end do we ask for it?
23. What are the fruits of the Spirit?
24. What is the way of truth?
25. What do we ask for all such as have erred or are deceived?
26. How many companies of Christian soldiers are named?
27. What is our prayer for such as do stand? for the weak-hearted? for them that fall?
28. What is our final prayer?
29. What brought suffering into the world?
30. What do we ask for those in danger, necessity, and tribulation?
31. Why do we specially commend to God travellers? women labouring of child? sick persons? young children? prisoners and captives?
32. What do we ask for fatherless children and widows?
33. Who are the desolate and oppressed? what do we ask for them?
34. What warrantry have we in praying for all men?
35. What do you understand by enemies, persecutors, and slanderers?
36. On what grounds do we pray for them?
37. What is our prayer for them?
38. What do you mean by the "kindly fruits of the earth?"
39. Which petition in the Lord's Prayer is here enlarged?

40. Explain what is meant by "true repentance."
41. Explain the difference between sins, negligences, and ignorances?
42. On what must amendment be based?
43. By what rule must we amend our lives?
44. Why do we pray to our Lord as the Lamb of God?
45. Why do we pray to Him as Christ?
46. What prayers do we make in these concluding versicles and responses?

IV.—THE SUPPLICATIONS.

1. When were the Supplications first used?
2. Why do we say them now?
3. How do they begin?
4. Of what does the Lord's Prayer consist as it stands in the Litany?
5. What authority have we for addressing God as our Father?
6. Why do we say "Which art in Heaven?"
7. For what do we pray in Petition I.?
8. How is Petition II. enlarged in the Burial Service?
9. Explain how God's Will may be fulfilled in us and by us.
10. To what do the first three Petitions refer, and to what the last four?
11. Explain Petition IV.
12. What commentary did our Lord give upon Petition V.?
13. Explain the meaning of "temptation" in its two senses.
14. What is meant in the Lord's Prayer by "evil?"
15. What is the meaning of "Amen?"
16. On what verse of the Psalms are the next versicle and response founded?
17. What is the meaning of "after" in them?
18. Why does the minister say "Let us pray" before the next prayer?

19. Whence is this prayer taken ?
20. What encouragement to prayer is mentioned in the introduction ?
21. What petitions does it contain ?
22. From whence are the ensuing versicles and responses taken ?
23. What is the Gloria Patri ?
24. Who are the enemies from whom we ask deliverance ?
25. By whom was Christ prayed to as Son of David when He was on earth ?
26. What are infirmities ?
27. Whence do man's infirmities arise ?
28. In what spirit should we pray for the removal of punishment ?
29. What is the history of the next prayer ?
30. What do you mean by praying "with one accord ?"
31. What promise does this prayer plead ?
32. What is the difference between desires and petitions ?
33. Why do we ask God to fulfil our prayers as may be most expedient for us ?
34. What do we ask with confidence ?
35. Explain the Benedictory Prayer.